Introducing Habitats

Water Habitats

Molly Aloian and Bobbie Kalman

Crabtree Publishing Company

www.crabtreebooks.com

Created by Bobbie Kalman

Dedicated by Candice Murphy
To my son Zach, whose strength and self-discipline allow him the freedom
to flow through life happily without arrogance! My love always, Mom

Editor-in-Chief
Bobbie Kalman

Writing team
Molly Aloian
Bobbie Kalman

Substantive editor
Kathryn Smithyman

Editors
Michael Hodge
Kelley MacAulay
Rebecca Sjonger

Design
Katherine Berti
Samantha Crabtree
    (cover and series logo)

Production coordinator
Heather Fitzpatrick

Photo research
Crystal Sikkens

Special thanks to
Jack Pickett and Karen Van Atte

Illustrations
Barbara Bedell: pages 10 (white fish, green fish, and coral), 14 (bottom), 15,
    32 (bottom right)
Katherine Berti: pages 10 (yellow fish and blue fish), 14 (top), 32 (top)
Bonna Rouse: pages 13 (sea star), 32 (bottom left)
Margaret Amy Salter: pages 13 (snail), 14 (middle)

Photographs
BigStockPhoto.com: Iris Abbott: page 27 (top); Paul Wolf: page 31
iStockphoto.com: pages 18 (bottom), 21 (bottom), 25, 28, 30
© Dwight Kuhn: page 22
Photo Researchers, Inc.: Richard R. Hansen: page 15
© Doug Perrine/Seapics.com: front cover
Other images by Corel, Creatas, Digital Stock, Digital Vision, and Photodisc

Library and Archives Canada Cataloguing in Publication

Aloian, Molly
    Water habitats / Molly Aloian & Bobbie Kalman.

(Introducing habitats)
ISBN-13: 978-0-7787-2949-5 (bound)
ISBN-10: 0-7787-2949-4 (bound)
ISBN-13: 978-0-7787-2977-8 (pbk.)
ISBN-10: 0-7787-2977-X (pbk.)

    1. Aquatic habitats--Juvenile literature. I. Kalman, Bobbie, date.
II. Title. III. Series.

QH541.5.W3A46 2006   j577.6   C2006-904085-0

Library of Congress Cataloging-in-Publication Data

Aloian, Molly.
    Water habitats / Molly Aloian & Bobbie Kalman.
        p. cm. -- (Introducing habitats)
    ISBN-13: 978-0-7787-2949-5 (rlb)
    ISBN-10: 0-7787-2949-4 (rlb)
    ISBN-13: 978-0-7787-2977-8 (pb)
    ISBN-10: 0-7787-2977-X (pb)
    1. Aquatic habitats--Juvenile literature. I. Kalman, Bobbie. II. Title.
III. Series.

QH541.5.W3A56 2007
577.6--dc22
                                                    2006021840

Crabtree Publishing Company

www.crabtreebooks.com   1-800-387-7650

Published in Canada
Crabtree Publishing
616 Welland Ave.
St. Catharines, ON
L2M 5V6

Published in the United States
Crabtree Publishing
PMB 59051
350 Fifth Avenue, 59th Floor
New York, New York 10118

Published in the United Kingdom
Crabtree Publishing
Maritime House
Basin Road North, Hove
BN41 1WR

Published in Australia
Crabtree Publishing
3 Charles Street
Coburg North
VIC 3058

Contents

Wonderful water!

All **living things** need water to stay alive. Plants and animals are living things. Plants need water to grow and to stay healthy. Animals need to drink water. Some animals swim and find food in water. This sea otter found food in water.

Water is everywhere

There is water everywhere! There is water in oceans, lakes, ponds, and rivers. Clouds are water in the sky. There is also water in **fog**. Fog is a cloud that is close to the ground.

Water habitats

A **habitat** is a place in nature. Plants live in habitats. Animals live in habitats, too. There are many kinds of water habitats. Different plants and animals live in the different water habitats.

Salt water and fresh water

The water in some water habitats is **salt water**. Salt water has a lot of salt in it. The water in other water habitats is **fresh water**. Fresh water has only a little salt in it. This sea slug lives in salt water.

Five oceans

Oceans are huge water habitats. They
are made up of salt water. There are five
oceans. The five oceans are the Atlantic
Ocean, the Pacific Ocean, the Indian Ocean,
the Arctic Ocean, and the Southern Ocean.
Find the oceans on this map of the world.

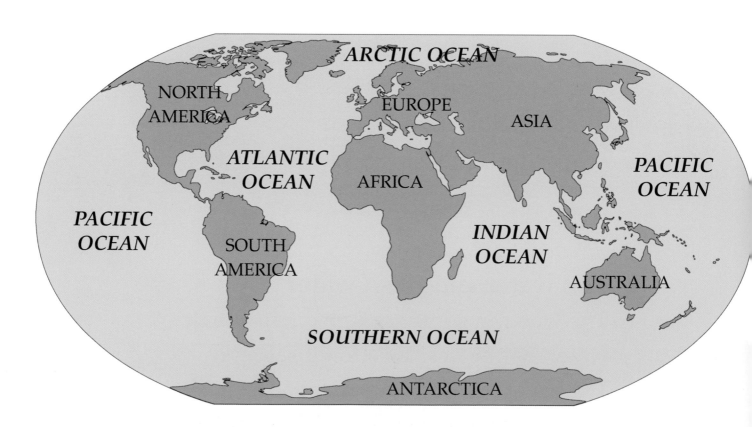

8

Warm or cold

Some oceans are in parts of the world that have hot weather. These oceans have warm water. Other oceans are in parts of the world that have cold weather. The water in these oceans is cold. This polar bear swims in the cold Arctic Ocean.

Colorful coral reefs

Warm oceans have **coral reefs**. Coral reefs are very colorful! Coral reefs look like huge groups of colorful plants. Coral reefs are not made up of plants, however. Coral reefs are made up of **corals**. Corals are groups of tiny animals called **coral polyps**.

Blending in

Many ocean animals live in coral reefs. Some of the animals have colorful bodies. Their bodies are the same colors as the corals. This stonefish's colorful body looks just like the corals around it. The stonefish blends in with the corals. It may not be seen by animals that want to eat it.

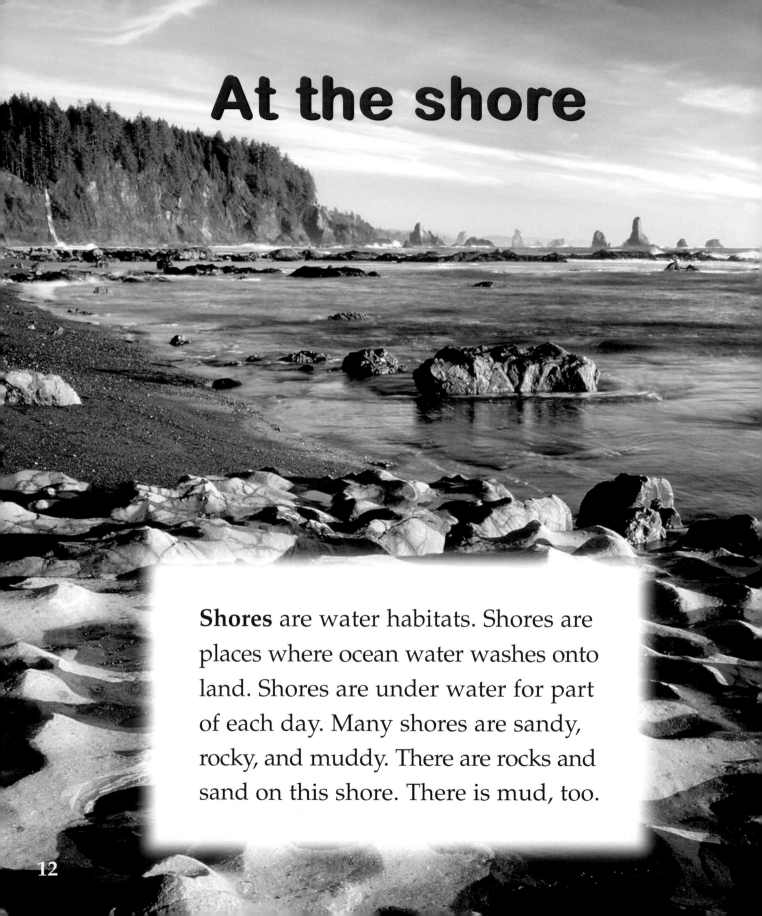

At the shore

Shores are water habitats. Shores are places where ocean water washes onto land. Shores are under water for part of each day. Many shores are sandy, rocky, and muddy. There are rocks and sand on this shore. There is mud, too.

Tide pools

Many shores have small pools of shallow water. These small pools are called **tide pools**. Tide pools never become dry. Plants and animals live in tide pools. This boy has found an insect in a tide pool. Sea stars and sea snails also live in tide pools.

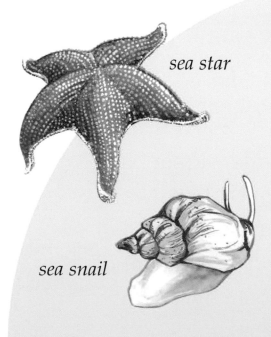

sea star

sea snail

13

Animals at the shore

A crab uses its legs to run away from animals that want to eat it.

A mussel has two shells that it can open and close.

Many animals live at shores. Birds, clams, crabs, shrimps, and mussels are animals that live at shores. These animals find plenty of food to eat in this habitat. Many water birds have long legs. When the birds stand in water looking for food, their bodies do not get wet.

Bird beaks

This egret is catching a shrimp to eat at a shore. It catches shrimp with its long beak. Its long beak is perfect for reaching shrimps in the water.

A lot of lakes

There are thousands of lakes on Earth!
Lakes are large bodies of water. There is land
all around lakes. The water in most lakes is
deep, but some lakes have shallow water.
This moose is standing in a shallow lake.

Fresh water

Lakes are freshwater habitats. Animals that need fresh water to stay alive spend time in or near lakes. Fish, birds, and other animals need fresh water to stay alive. This eagle is trying to catch a fish in a lake.

Life in lakes

Many animals live in lakes. Trout and bass are two kinds of fish that live in lakes. Crayfish live on the bottoms of lakes. They search for food to eat in the mud.

Finding food

Many birds live in habitats with cold winter weather. The birds cannot stay alive in the cold. When the weather gets cold, the birds leave their habitats. They fly to warmer habitats. During their long journeys, the birds stop at lakes to rest and to find food.

Small ponds

Ponds are water habitats that are smaller than lakes. Like lakes, ponds also have land around them. The water in many ponds is shallow. It is also **still**. Still water moves very little. These geese are standing in a still pond.

Pond plants

Plants grow in ponds and near the edges of ponds. Animals eat parts of the plants. Moths drink **nectar** from pond flowers. Nectar is a sweet liquid found in flowers.

Swimming in ponds

Many kinds of animals live in pond habitats. Some animals live in the water. Fish and **tadpoles** live in the water. Tadpoles are baby frogs. This tadpole is a great swimmer!

Along the pond

Many kinds of birds spend time in ponds. This bird made a home near the edge of a pond. Its home is called a **nest**. It will lay eggs inside the nest. Baby birds will hatch from the eggs.

Moving river water

Rivers have fresh water. The water in rivers is not still, as the water in ponds is. The water in rivers flows. Some rivers have **waterfalls**. A waterfall is a stream of water that falls from a high place.

Super swimmers

Salmon are fish that swim in rivers. They are strong swimmers. Salmon can swim against the flow of the water in rivers. Salmon can even swim up waterfalls! This bear is catching a salmon as it swims up a waterfall.

River animals

These hippopotamuses are river animals. They live and find food in their river habitat. They are swimming in a group. The group of hippos is called a **herd**.

Living in rivers

Many animals live in rivers. River otters and crocodiles live in rivers. They swim from place to place searching for food to eat.

*A river otter's fur is **waterproof**. Waterproof fur stays dry in water.*

A crocodile has sharp teeth for biting into fish, birds, and turtles.

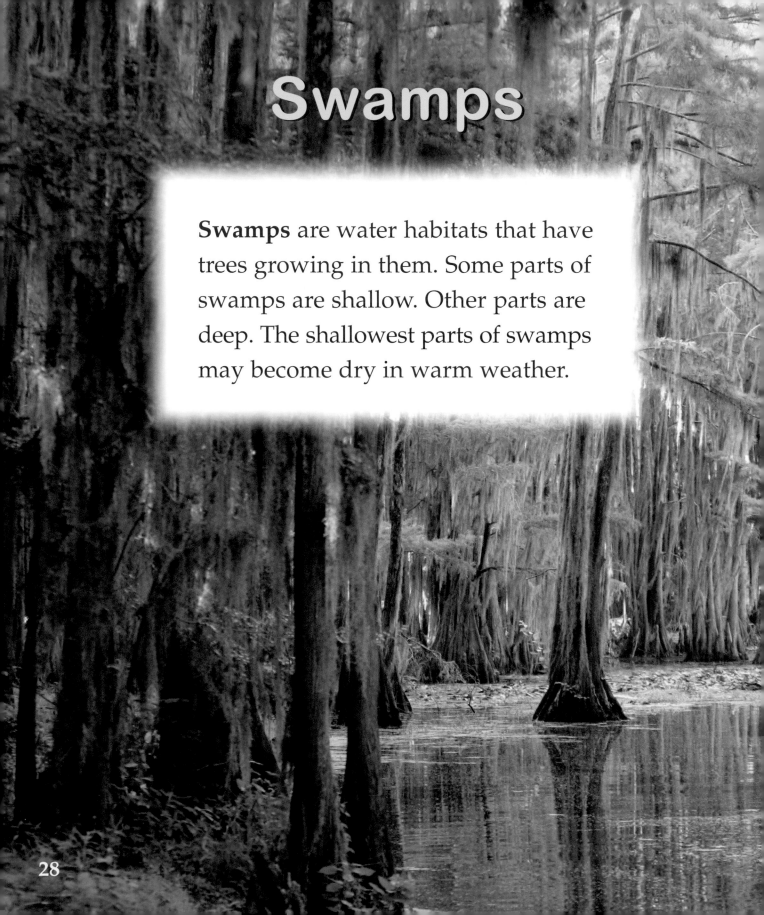

Swamps

Swamps are water habitats that have trees growing in them. Some parts of swamps are shallow. Other parts are deep. The shallowest parts of swamps may become dry in warm weather.

In the trees

Oak, maple, elm, and cypress trees grow
in swamps. Many birds make nests in the
tree branches. The birds find food and water
in the swamp below the trees. These great
egrets have made a nest in a swamp tree.

Living in swamps

Many swamp animals live in water.
Others live on the wet land around
swamps. Some animals live both in
water and on land. This snapping
turtle spends some time in water
and some time on land.

Swamp alligators

Alligators are large swamp animals. They swim in swamps looking for fish, turtles, and snakes to eat. If a swamp becomes dry, the alligators move to other water habitats.

Words to know and Index

animals
pages 4, 6, 10, 11, 13, 14, 17, 18, 21, 22, 26, 27, 30, 31

food
pages 4, 14, 18, 19, 26, 27, 29

coral reefs
pages 10-11

habitats
pages 6, 7, 8, 12, 14, 17, 19, 20, 22, 26, 28, 31

herd
page 26

nests
pages 23, 29

plants
pages 4, 6, 10, 13, 21

swimming
pages 4, 9, 22, 25, 26, 27, 31

Other index words